© Wyatt North Publishing, LLC 2019

Chapter 1: The Hundred Years' War

Over a period of more than one hundred years, five generations of kings from the English House of Plantagenet and the French House of Valois fought over which dynasty had the right to the throne of the Kingdom of France, the largest kingdom in Western Europe. Five generations of kings and their assorted allies engaged in armed conflict from 1337 to 1453. During that time, chivalry waned and both England and France developed strong national identities that took precedence over allegiances to multiple smaller feudal entities.

The House of Plantagenet

Why did the English House of Plantagenet claim the right to the French throne? The answer lies in the Plantagenet family's French roots. For generations, Plantagenet kings also held French titles and lands, or fiefdoms, which made them subservient to the kings of France—even though at some points, the English held more land in France than the French king did. This was a source of much discord between the two royal houses. The French monarchs sought to strip French lands from the Plantagenets to stem the growth of English power, until by 1337, the only English holding remaining in France was Gascony.

The House of Valois

When King Charles IV of France died without any close male relatives in 1328, his closest male relative was his nephew, Edward III, whose mother was the deceased king's sister, Isabella of France. The succession to the French throne was contended because of a legal principle, established in French law a dozen years earlier, prohibiting the accession of a woman. Isabella claimed the crown for her son, but the French rejected the idea of being ruled by Edward III, who was regarded as English. Instead, Philip, Count of Valois, a cousin on the deceased king's father's side, was named King Philip VI, and the crown passed to the House of Valois. Later disagreements between King Philip VI of France and King Edward III of England led to the confiscation of Edward's lands in France, and Edward renewed the House of Plantagenet's claim to the French throne. Thus began the war that would last for more than a century.

A Multi-Phase War

Several English victories early in the war gave the English the necessary confidence to continue devoting resources to the conflict for many decades. However, they were fighting on foreign soil against the greater resources of the French. Before the House of Valois gained ultimate victory, there were temporary truces that historians now use to divide the Hundred Years' War into three phases: 1) the Edwardian War (1337–1360); 2) the Caroline War (1369–1389); and 3) the Lancastrian War (1415–1453). Historians have also included several other European conflicts occurring during roughly the same period, under the umbrella term "Hundred Years' War," making it the longest armed conflict in European history. Among these are the War of the Breton Succession (1341–1365), the Castilian Civil War (1366–1369), the War of the Two Peters that took place in Aragon (1356–1369), and the crisis in Portugal (1383–1385). Both the French and the English took advantage of these conflicts to further their respective cause.

The Battle of Agincourt

One of the most momentous events of the Hundred Years' War, the Battle of Agincourt, which took place when St. Joan was a little girl, was a humiliating defeat for the French. Young King Henry V of England sailed to Normandy with 11,000 troops and laid siege to the town of Harfleur. Half of his troops fell to disease or died in battle before Harfleur surrendered after five weeks. While marching his troops back to the coast to return to England, Henry encountered a French force of more than 20,000 at Agincourt.

Henry's army, exhausted and greatly reduced in numbers from their long siege of Harfleur, found an unexpected advantage in the flat terrain of the 1,000-yard battlefield, which lay between two expansive wooded areas where large-scale maneuvers by the French were impossible. Moreover, the French soldiers wore heavy armor, which made it difficult to slog across the muddy battlefield. And the English were using a new kind of crossbow, with a much longer range than the French were expecting. They also had time to plant a line of sharp, pointed stakes in the ground in front of them, which protected them from the English cavalrymen. Weighed down by their heavy armor, the French knights soon found themselves crowded together in the small clearing, without enough room to swing their swords and fight effectively in close quarters. Henry's troops, lightly armored and able to move quickly, surged forward and mowed down the French.

When the battle was over, 6,000 of the 20,000 French troops were dead, while Henry had only lost a few over 400 men. To this day, the English defeat of a force that outnumbered it by more than three to one is considered one of the greatest military triumphs of all time. After a few more English victories over the French, the latter finally recognized Henry V's claim to the French throne, but he fell ill and died only two years later. The humiliation of the defeat at Agincourt fueled French opposition to the English presence in France for decades to come.

Historical Significance of the Hundred Years' War

The Hundred Years' War changed the way war was waged. Feudal armies led by aristocratic knights, who owed their allegiance to specific noblemen and were called to combat only in times of conflict, were replaced by standing armies of professional troops, recruited from the general populace, that could be mobilized on short notice. Heavily armored cavalry that engaged in close combat with swords, pikes, and lances gave way to artillery that inflicted damage from a distance, alongside a variety of new weapons and tactics.

From a political and social perspective, what started out as a conflict between two rival dynasties gave rise to an unprecedented sense of nationalism among both the French and the English. The Hundred Years' War was fought primarily on French soil, and the French citizenry suffered the consequences of prolonged sieges, famine, deadly epidemics, and marauding free-companies of mostly foreign mercenaries. These were most prevalent during the periods of truce between long periods of active hostilities, when professional soldiers without useful civilian skills were unemployed and turned to pillaging throughout the countryside. All of these factors contributed to drastic reductions of the French population.

English civilians were less affected by the immediate effects of prolonged armed conflict, but the political impact of the war was significant. The English nobility grew resentful at the loss of their landholdings in France and at the monarchy's desire to funnel more and more money into waging a losing war. Internal disagreements between the House of Plantagenet and the House of York would lead to a serious of English civil wars, known as the War of the Roses, which began only two short years after the end of the Hundred Years' War.

If it were not for the Hundred Years' War, Joan of Arc might have lived out her life as an obscure French peasant. Instead, she played a major role in it and will be remembered forever as an inspiring symbol of faith, selflessness, and courage.

Chapter 2: Joan's Early Life

the early life of Jeanne d'Arc, or Joan of Arc in English. She is believed to have been born in or around 1412, after seventy-five years of the ongoing conflict with England known as the Hundred Years' War. During Joan's childhood and youth, the English had the upper hand in the conflict. One of five children of a tenant farmer, she was born and raised in the village of Domrémy, in northeastern France, close to lands occupied by the English and their French allies led by the Duke of Burgundy. We can surmise much based on these few facts and historical records documenting what life was like in France in the early fifteenth century. The other key source of information about Joan's early life is the testimony of the people of the village of Domrémy during the trial of rehabilitation held twenty-five years after her martyrdom.

Joan's Religious Formation

Johannes Gutenberg's invention of moveable type occurred about a decade after Joan's martyrdom. During her lifetime, the vast majority of common people were illiterate. Only the wealthy and noble had access to books, which were laboriously copied by hand by scribes, primarily monks. Joan never learned to read and write, so what she knew of the Bible and the teachings of the Church she learned by attending Mass with her family and listening to the instruction provided by her mother, Isabelle Romée. It was in the village church that Joan saw the images of St. Michael, St. Catherine of Alexandria, and St. Margaret of Antioch almost daily. These were the three saints Joan identified as the divine messengers whose voices inspired and guided her.

In her testimony, Joan's mother said, "I had a daughter born in lawful wedlock who grew up amid the fields and pastures. I had her baptized and confirmed, and brought her up in the fear of God. I taught her respect for the traditions of the Church … I succeeded so well that she spent much of her time in church, and after having gone to confession, she received the sacrament of the Eucharist every month. Because the people suffered so much, she had a great compassion for them in her heart and despite her youth she would fast and pray for them with great devotion and fervor." Similar testimony was provided by local church officials, friends, and relatives, all of whom confirmed Joan's piety and her love for God. Her godfather testified that she was "well and properly brought up in the faith and good conduct and so much so that nearly all the inhabitants of Domrémy loved her." According to the testimony of a neighboring farmer, "She was good and simple, and went often to the churches and holy shrines. When she was in the fields, she used to drop to her knees and pray every time she heard the church bells toll." Joan's religious foundation and devotion to God were evident in every aspect of her brief life.

Social and Cultural Influences

The early fifteenth century was a period of transition between the Late Middle Ages and the Early Renaissance. During the Middle Ages, European society was broadly divided into social classes referred to as "estates." At the top of the heap was the First Estate, consisting of high-ranking clergy—cardinals, archbishops, bishops, abbots, and so on. The First Estate had great influence over the uneducated masses and also ruled over large landholdings belonging to the Church. The Second Estate consisted of the landed aristocracy living in the countryside. The descendants of feudal warlords, they still maintained their own armies or hired large numbers of mercenaries to protect their interests against the increasing power of multiple monarchies. The Third Estate comprised the new class of bourgeoisie. These mayors, merchants, and master artisans were striving to increase their political influence and power. And then there was everyone else—

lawyers, teachers, journeymen and apprentices in a wide variety of trades, unskilled laborers, and the peasants who worked the land in the countryside. Joan's family and most members of her community were in this last category—members of no class or estate.

The life of the typical fifteenth-century peasant (from the French word *paysan*, which referred to anyone living in the countryside) was probably not the way we've seen it depicted. Judging from literature and films set in the 1400s, we've formed an image of peasants as dirty and ignorant—little more than slaves—living cheek-by-jowl in vermin-infested hovels. Archeological evidence, however, contradicts that image. Excavated fifteenth-century homes in rural European villages were generally well-constructed of wood and fieldstone, many of them with private upper rooms for sleeping. Archeologists have discovered evidence of locked doors and chests, tablecloths and candle holders, decorative pottery, coins, and recreational items such as dice, chess sets, cards, musical instruments, and boards for playing ninemen's morris, a strategy board game dating back to the Roman Empire. There were outdoor privies and evidence of herbs being used on bedding to repel insects, all of which suggest a better standard of living during Joan's lifetime than one might imagine.

Joan's father, Jacques d'Arcy, was a tenant farmer living on and working lands owned by a landlord. Serfdom, a system under which agricultural workers, or serfs, were legally bound to the land, wasn't officially abolished until the French Revolution, but had been in decline in France for a century or more. Tenant farmers negotiated their own contracts with their landlords, and there is reason to believe that the d'Arcy family was reasonably comfortable by the standards of the day.

Multiple Allegiances and an Atmosphere of Conflict

The charges against Joan identified her as coming from "Domrémy on the Meuse, in the diocese of Toul, in the bailiwick of Chaumont-en-Bassigny, in the provostry of Monteclaire and Andelot." There has long been controversy surrounding the "ownership" of Joan, who grew up in an area where people typically had multiple, conflicting allegiances. Though it's unknown what Jacques d'Arcy's sentiments were or how they might have influenced young Joan, it's certain that she was no stranger to the turmoil associated with warring loyalties.

Domrémy was located in northeastern France, in what was essentially the frontier between the lands controlled by the French and those occupied by the English and their Burgundian allies. Bordering on the duchies of Bar and Lorraine, the westernmost parts of the Holy Roman Empire, the residents of Domrémy were sharply divided in their loyalties. A branch of the Meuse River bisected the village, and those living on the south bank were serfs of a local lord who was a vassal of the Duke of Bar. Households on the northern bank belonged to freedman and were under the administration of the nearby fortified town of Vaucouleurs in the bailiwick of Chaumont, a direct possession of the French crown. The course of the river apparently shifted over the centuries, and it's unclear whether the d'Arcy home was located to the north or the south of that dividing line.

During her childhood, the part of France where Joan grew up saw more armed conflict and violence than any other, apart from Paris and the Seine basin, but not all of it was due to the war against the English and Burgundians. Around the time of Joan's birth, the Duke of Lorraine tried to seize a town just upstream on the Meuse from Domrémy and failed after some bloody fighting. Professional soldiers also roamed the countryside on behalf of the French crown, pillaging and plundering villages that sympathized with the Burgundians, who made occasional incursions into the area. The residents of Domrémy were no strangers to armed conflict, and they were sometimes required to flee their homes to avoid the Burgundian threat.

In 1423, only a couple of years before Joan began hearing her divine "Voices," her father was serving as dean of Domrémy, which made him responsible for protecting the village, distributing food stores, and collecting taxes. This gave Joan firsthand knowledge of the impact of the violence being inflicted on her neighbors. When the governor-general of the Barrois laid siege to a town close to Domrémy that was being used as a base of operations by the large mercenary band, violence hit even closer to home for Joan. During that siege, the husband of her cousin and close friend was killed. And two years later, a Domrémy resident, known locally as a bandit who sympathized with the Burgundians, was falsely accused of stealing livestock and was murdered without being arrested or convicted. (Thirty years later, another Domrémy resident confessed to and was pardoned for the crime.) Joan, with her strict moral upbringing, would have seen this as a true injustice.

When Joan was about 16, pro-Burgundian forces led by the governor of Champagne laid waste to villages around the town of Vaucouleurs, which was loyal to the French crown. Several villages, including Domrémy, were put to the torch. The church next door to Joan's home was burned, and the d'Arcy family, along with the rest of the villagers, were evacuated. At her trial, Joan spoke of frequently leading the family's livestock to safety, out of Domrémy and away from marauding soldiers. Suspicion, hostility, instability, and the ever-present threat of violence were constants in Joan's life. But all of these elements were anathema to her natural inclination toward order and unity.

Chapter 3: Joan's Voices

The First Encounters

According to Joan, who was unsure of her actual date of birth, she was about thirteen when she first heard the voices that she believed to have been sent by God. Her insistence that they were of divine origin was the central point of contention during her trial and ultimately led to her martyrdom. Though she later maintained that the voices instructed her to fight the English and help the dauphin, Charles of Valois, gain the French throne—which had been denied to him by the English Plantagenets after the death of his father, Charles VI—that wasn't their original purpose, according to Joan.

She testified that at first, their message was to conduct herself appropriately, attend church, and lead a pious life. But her description of whom the voices belonged to, what their purpose was, what they said, and whether they had a physical presence evolved from the first encounter until the end of her life. Over a period of roughly two years, Joan continued to hear unearthly voices, which were usually accompanied by a bright light. Their arrival often coincided with the ringing of church bells, and Joan was eventually able to see as well as hear them. During that time, the messages escalated: At first, they told her to go to Mass and be charitable to those in need. Later, they would command her to relieve the siege of Orleans, escort the dauphin to Reims to be anointed and crowned as king of France, and lead his troops in driving out the English. Joan dutifully followed all of the instructions she was given by the voices.

All that is known about Joan's experiences with her voices comes from her testimony during her trial and interrogations and from one letter written before the trial by Percival de Boulainvilliers, courtier of Charles VII to the Duke of Milan, to whom he was related by marriage. He recounted Joan's description of encountering a certain youth while running footraces with her friends in the fields of Domrémy. He told her to run home to help her mother, but when she got there, her mother denied having sent anyone to fetch her. When she returned to her friends, a shimmering silver cloud obscured her vision and she heard a voice emanating from the cloud tell her, "Joan, you must lead another life and perform wondrous deeds; for you are she whom the King of Heaven has chosen to bring reparation to the kingdom of France and help and protection to King Charles."

This appears to have been an educated man's courtly version of the explanation Joan would later give during her trial. At the second public session she described herself as being in her father's garden on a sunny summer day when she first heard a voice coming from the direction of the village church and said that it was accompanied by a "great light." According to the trial transcript, Joan explained, "When I was thirteen years old, I had a Voice from God to help me govern my conduct. And the first time I was very fearful. And came this Voice, about the hour of noon, in the summer-time, in my father's garden; I had not fasted on the eve preceding that day." Saying that she had not fasted the previous day was apparently intended to allay any suspicions that she was hallucinating from hunger.

The Angels

Joan described what she heard as a "worthy voice," but said she did not recognize it as belonging to an angel until she heard it for the third time, when it instructed her and helped her find the king. This was the encounter of which her relative wrote in his letter to the Duke of Milan. When pressed by prosecutors about her encounter with that angel, Joan became impatient with the questioning. She also spoke of Charles as having had his own revelations and apparitions and said that those accompanying her knew the voice was sent to her by God. She said specifically that they "saw and knew the voice too." Shortly after referring to a singular "voice," she used the plural for the first time, stating that "the king and several others, including the Duke of Bourbon, heard and saw **them**."

Two days later, during the third public session, there was again some ambiguity as to whether Joan's counsel came from a single voice or from three, and whether the voice was that of an angel or a saint. It was not until the fourth public session that Joan named St. Michael, St. Catherine of Alexandria, and St. Margaret of Antioch, gave a physical description of them, and said that she had God's permission to share this information. She then identified St. Michael as the first to have visited her in the fields of Domrémy. At several points during that session, Joan emphasized the comfort the voices brought her, and was pressed again and again to claim that she saw the saints and interacted with them "corporeally and in reality." She finally answered, "I saw them with my bodily eyes as well as I see you; and when they left me, I wept; and I would have had them take me with them, too."

Physical Manifestations

During the final two public sessions and the interrogations in her cell, Joan gave evasive and often contradictory answers to questions about her physical experience with the saints. She seemed to sense the trap that was being laid for her, but lying about her divine counsel was anathema to her. What descriptive information she did provide reflected the iconography and images used by the Church in the religious education of illiterate congregants. Her final cross-examination began with the familiar questions about the physical appearance of St. Michael as Joan had seen him. By the end of the questioning, an exhausted Joan repeatedly answered "yes" to questions about her voices, giving the prosecutors reason to pronounce her guilty of the most serious charges against her. In the end, it was not Joan's specific actions, but rather her claims that they were divinely inspired, that led to the guilty verdict.

Joan's inquisitors and prosecutors found it incredulous that God would have chosen Joan. Consequently, the question of the reality of Joan's voices dominated her trial and continues to be a subject of debate centuries later. Heresy and witchcraft were the most serious charges against her, and the prosecutors set out to prove the voices to be those of Satan, Belial, and Behemoth.

Though the nature of Joan's voices was the main issue at her trial, it was barely mentioned during her trial of rehabilitation, which started in 1455, fourteen years after her death at the stake. Her supporters who testified at the trial of rehabilitation did not mention the identity of her voices but rather described her as having received "counsel from God." Her enemies and prosecutors at her original trial, however, were obsessed with the identity and physical manifestation of her voices.

Some experts believe that Joan suffered auditory and visual hallucinations stemming from a neurological or psychiatric condition like schizophrenia or a brain tumor. Others blamed drinking unpasteurized milk, which causes bovine tuberculosis, characterized by seizures and dementia. Some simply believe that she lied. Though many have suggested that Joan's voices were merely projections of her own thoughts and imaginings, to her they were decidedly external to her own physical existence. She saw and heard the three saints with her physical senses. On two occasions, she claimed that she couldn't hear them clearly because of ambient noise.

Joan's Loyalty to Her Voices

Joan was obedient and loyal to her voices. From their first instructions to her regarding her conduct, Joan announced her determination to remain a virgin. She made it clear for the remainder of her life that she had no interest in men as anything other than comrades in arms, and she insisted on being called "La Pucelle"—the Maid—as a reminder of her virginal status. During her trial, she further demonstrated her loyalty to her voices by absolving them of responsibility for the predicament in which she found herself. When asked whether she followed their instructions in everything she did, she gave a testy reply: "Everything *good* that I did."

What is most important to understand about Joan's voices is that they confirmed and deepened her faith in God. And it was her deep faith in God that gave her—an insignificant, uneducated peasant girl—the power to do incredible things.

Chapter 4: Joan Answers the Call

Joan Seeks an Introduction to the Dauphin

Though Joan insisted that, at first, the voices she heard merely counseled her on her behavior and guided her in becoming a better person, they eventually revealed to her their true purpose in visiting her. In May of 1428, when Joan was 16, they conveyed to her God's command that she take the dauphin Charles, rightful heir to the French throne, to Reims for his coronation, and then drive the English out of France. To be admitted to see Charles, she knew she would first have to go to Robert de Baudricourt, commander of the dauphin's army in the town of Vaucouleurs, not far from Joan's home in Domrémy. She couldn't expect simply to present herself to Charles, announce her mission, and expect to be taken seriously. She needed Baudricourt's introduction and endorsement.

Her uncle, Durand Laxart, escorted Joan to Vaucouleurs, where she made her case to Baudricourt. She asked him for armed soldiers to escort her to Chinon, on the Loire River, the makeshift seat of the French royal court at the time. Baudricourt laughed at the idea of a young peasant girl thinking she could lead an army and sent her home, saying that her father should give her a whipping.

Back in Domrémy, the voices persisted despite Joan's protests that she was merely a poor girl who couldn't even ride a horse, let alone fight. However, it appears that during this time, Joan learned how to ride on a horse her cousin bought for her for twelve francs, a sum that was later reimbursed by Robert de Baudricourt. The voices told Joan it was God's command they were conveying. During her trial, when Joan was questioned about leaving home without her parents' permission, she testified that she left at God's command, but later sent a letter to her parents and was forgiven by them.

When Joan returned to Vaucouleurs a few months later, in January, 1429, her impassioned plea won over two of Baudricourt's soldiers, Jean de Metz and Bertrand de Poulengy, who would remain her staunch supporters. They arranged for her to meet with Baudricourt. During that meeting, Joan predicted that the French would soon suffer a crushing defeat. A few days later, messengers arrived to report the French defeat at the Battle of Rouvray (Battle of the Herrings) near Orléans. Baudricourt now feared that Orleans, the last remaining French stronghold on the Loire—not far from Rouvray—would soon fall. That fear, along with Joan's prescience about the defeat at Rouvray, gave credence to her claims of divine revelations and persuaded Baudricourt to give her an escort of three soldiers to take her to the dauphin in Chinon.

Joan Meets the Dauphin

At the suggestion of two members of her escort, Joan donned male clothing for the first time for the journey from Vaucouleurs to Chinon, which took them through hostile Burgundian territory. While her escort regarded this as a sensible precaution, such "cross-dressing" ultimately became one of the most serious charges against Joan.

Joan and her escort reached Chinon on March 6, 1429, and she was granted an audience with the dauphin two days later. Charles apparently had some idea of why Joan was there, because he arranged a "test" of her discernment by disguising himself as one of his courtiers. Joan identified him as the dauphin right away (at her trial she said that her voices led her to recognize him) and was able to convince him of the validity of her mission. Her request for troops, however, was opposed by the ministers of the court, especially the influential Georges de la Trémoille, who had the dauphin's ear and insisted that she was either crazy or conniving.

Joan was sent to Poitiers, where a commission of theologians were to examine her and report their findings to Charles. After three weeks of intense questioning, the commission found Joan to be "honest, good, and virtuous" and recommended that Charles allow her to serve him. Upon her return to Chinon, Joan was granted another audience with the dauphin, during which she told him that divine voices had commanded her to fight the English. If the French were victorious, she explained, she would escort Charles to Reims, where all French kings were crowned, for his own coronation.

Joan's Mission to Break the Siege at Orléans

Charles and his ministers decided to allow Joan to lead a small force into battle at Orléans, a city that had been under siege by the English for some time. The dauphin's mother-in-law, Yolande of Aragon, was already committed to financing an attempt to break the siege, so it was a simple enough matter to allow Joan to ride at the front of the army. The French Crown paid for her suit of white armor, but her horse and sword and most of the equipment for her personal entourage were all donated.

Joan asked for a banner to be made for her and described in great detail what she envisioned: a figure of God the Father being presented a fleur-de-lis, the French monarchy's royal symbol, by two kneeling angels. The banner bore the words "Jesus Maria," representing Jesus and his mother. With her dark hair cut short, the Joan that led the troops toward Orléans looked like a handsome young lad. From that point on, Joan called herself simply "La Pucelle," which means "The Maid." She chose the name to emphasize the fact that she remained a virgin in obedience to instructions from her voices, and she intended to die a virgin. "La Pucelle" is the name by which her troops knew her.

Though Joan was an impressive sight riding at the head of the army in her gleaming white armor, she knew nothing of war or military strategy. Why then, one might wonder, was she entrusted to lead the expedition to break the siege at Orléans? Historians have argued that the French were so demoralized after years of military defeats, and with the dauphin's hope of gaining the French throne growing dimmer by the day, that they saw it as the only option left to them. Another possibility is that Joan's arrival on the scene came not long after a prophecy made by Marie d'Arignon, a known visionary, about an "armed woman" who would soon arrive to save the French. One of the theologians who examined Joan at Poitiers was convinced that Joan was that armed woman and shared his conviction with the commission.

During her trial, Joan was pressured to explain why Charles so readily agreed to her request. The apparent aim was to elicit an admission of divine intervention that would serve as further evidence of heresy. Though she resisted giving the prosecutors what they were seeking, she eventually started speaking of Charles being given a crown by an angelic messenger, though the details changed as she told and retold the story. Regardless, it certainly made no military sense to rely on an illiterate teenaged peasant girl, who claimed to be following instructions from God, to lead the army into battle at Orléans.

What nobody counted on was how inspired the troops were by Joan's courage and deep faith. Following her banner, the French soldiers broke through the English line encircling Orléans and rode into the city on April 29, which emboldened the French troops garrisoned there. On May 8, they captured the English fort outside of the city, and the siege of Orléans was broken. Though Joan did not fight, she was a conspicuous target in her white armor, and an English archer's arrow wounded her in the shoulder. She would be wounded one more time during her brief military career, taking a crossbow bolt to the thigh during her unsuccessful attempt to liberate Paris.

Military Success

Joan had no taste for blood. One contemporary report described her attempt to avoid violence during the siege of Orléans. She is said to have dictated an impassioned plea to the English troops to withdraw without bloodshed. She tied the letter to an arrow and had a French archer shoot it into the English encampment. Needless to say, the enemy did not retreat. Their response came in a cry that spread through the English army: "News from the whore of the French Armagnacs!"

Joan led the French army into a few more battles along the Loire River, defeating the English each time, until the road to Reims had been cleared. She insisted that the dauphin be taken to Reims immediately for his coronation, just as she had been instructed by her divine voices. On July 17, 1429, the dauphin was crowned King Charles VII in the cathedral of Reims, as Joan looked on proudly.

Chapter 5: Joan the Warrior

Joan's Short Temper

Contrary to popular belief, the dauphin did not install Joan as the commander of any French army. She was accorded the status of a knight and given a squire, Jean d'Aulon, and a page, Louis de Coutes, and she was assigned a personal escort of an undetermined number of soldiers. Though she often rode at the front of the army, personal banner flying, she had the same freelance status as other "warlord" knights. That said, she had no qualms about chewing out the most prestigious of them when they angered her.

Many witnesses at Joan's trial of rehabilitation recounted stories of Joan's personal conduct, describing her as a force to be reckoned with. Knights who used profane language or didn't attend Mass, or whose conduct Joan found indecent, were in for a tongue lashing. She had no patience with anyone who questioned her strategy or failed to stand up to the English. One witness testified that she had slapped a Scottish soldier fighting alongside the French for eating stolen meat. Others said that she had ended the practice of mistresses and prostitutes traveling with the army by driving them away at sword-point. Even those who were impressed by her deep faith acknowledged her short temper and sharp tongue, which she most often loosed on those she found lacking in piety. Her page, Louis de Coutes, testified: "She was angry when she heard anyone blaspheming God's name or anyone swearing. I heard her reprimand my lord Duke of Alencon several times for swearing or uttering some blasphemy. On the whole, nobody in the army would have dared to swear or blaspheme in front of her for fear of a reprimand from her."

Joan's Spiritual and Military Leadership

Joan's army chaplain testified at her trial of rehabilitation that she was determined to improve the spiritual condition of the troops. When Joan led them into battle, she would have the priests who were traveling with the army march in the front ranks, singing in praise to God. It was also her custom to have all of the priests assemble around her banner in the morning and again in the evening to sing hymns praising the Blessed Mary. Only the soldiers who had confessed that day were allowed to attend.

While she undoubtedly deserved her reputation for spiritual leadership, there is little evidence that Joan played any real role in developing military strategy or serving as anything more than an inspirational figurehead. According to evidence presented at the rehabilitation hearings, Joan was never granted a role in the army's council, as she had requested. Nor was she officially in command of the army at Orléans. The success of the troops was attributed to divine intervention through Joan's contact with her voices.

Jean de Dunois, the illegitimate son of the Duke of Orléans, was in command of the French troops and led them on an approach to the city that took them along the left bank of the Beauce River. Joan argued that her voices commanded an approach from the right bank, but Dunois overruled her because of the placement of English camps. Approaching from the left bank meant that troops and provisions would have to be ferried across the river, but when they reached the point of embarkation, the winds were so strongly against them that they couldn't launch the boats. Joan was furious. At the rehabilitation trial, Dunois repeated what Joan had said to him: "You thought you had deceived me, but it is you who have deceived yourselves, for I am bringing you better help than ever you got from any soldier or any city. It is the help of the King of Heaven." According to his testimony, at that very moment the wind shifted and made it possible to cross the river. It was this incident that convinced him of Joan's connection to God and her divine mission.

The English defeat at Orléans was widely regarded as miraculous. Nobody claimed that it was due to any military expertise on Joan's part. The poet Alain Chartier wrote: "Here is she who seems not to issue from any place on earth, but rather sent by Heaven to sustain with head and shoulders a France fallen to the ground. O astonishing virgin!" It was not until the rehabilitation trial that Joan was credited with any military prowess, when she was praised for her placement of artillery. In fact, Raoul de Gaucourt, the bailiff of Orléans, actively argued against the impulsiveness Joan exhibited in demanding that the French pursue the retreating English troops after they were routed from the city. At one point, he stood at the city gates and attempted to stop her from leading the troops through them.

It is highly unlikely that Joan was an active combatant in any of the battles to take back the forts the English occupied on the outskirts of Orléans. Most of the fighting was hand-to-hand combat, fought to the death. At her trial, Joan denied having killed anyone. Her preferred mode of operation was to attempt to put the fear of God into the English and their

Burgundian allies, warning them beforehand to retreat or face His wrath. Prior to the French assault on Orléans, she dictated a letter to the English commanders leading the siege of the city:

"Surrender to the Maid sent hither, by God the King of Heaven, the keys of all the good towns you have taken and laid waste in France. She comes in God's name to establish the Blood Royal, ready to make peace if you agree to abandon France and repay what you have taken. And you, archers, comrades in arms, gentles and others, who are before the town of Orléans, retire in God's name to your own country. If you do not, expect to hear tidings from the Maid who will shortly come upon you to your very great hurt. And to you, King of England, if you do not do thus, I am a chieftain of war and whenever I meet your followers in France, I will drive them out; if they will not obey, I will put them all to death ... I am sent here in God's name, the King of Heaven, to drive you body for body out of all France ... You will not withhold the Kingdom of France from God, the King of King's, Blessed Mary's son. The King Charles, the true inheritor, will possess it, for God wills it and has revealed it through the Maid, and he will enter Paris with a good company."

At her trial, Joan denied having called herself a chieftain of war, and there is no real evidence that she actually did serve in that capacity.

Joan's Dwindling Influence

The coronation of the dauphin as Charles VII on July 17, 1429, marked the high point of Joan's influence. Against her advice, Charles began his withdrawal to the Loire. After a few minor skirmishes, he signed a truce with the Duke of Burgundy in late August, agreeing to a cessation of hostilities until Christmas. At the end of September, Charles disbanded the French army, which infuriated Joan, who had not accomplished her mission of driving the English out of France. In a letter to the people of Reims, Joan said that the truce was so little to her liking that she didn't know if she would keep it and that if she did, it would only be to maintain the honor of the king. Within a month, without the support or presence of the king, she was attacking Paris, which was held by the Burgundians. Though she expected the Parisians to rise up and join in the fight, they did not. She was seriously wounded in the unsuccessful attempt, and her reputation suffered for having made the attempt on Our Lady's birthday.

The truce held through the winter, which Joan spent recovering at court, but with her reputation and status much diminished. Hostilities resumed in the spring, but as a freelance commander, Joan was finding it increasingly difficult to raise money for the series of skirmishes and minor battles she led against the English and Burgundians with little success.

On May 23, 1430, Joan's military career came to an abrupt end with her capture during a skirmish outside the town of Compiègne, which was under siege by the Burgundians.

Chapter 6: A Political Pawn

The Capture of Joan of Arc

In the spring of 1430, hostilities resumed after the winter truce between the French and English. Joan, who had been seriously wounded by a crossbow bolt to the thigh during the failed attempt to retake Paris a few months earlier, was now recovered and rode off to Compiegne to lead a sortie against the Burgundian forces besieging the town. A few hours after arriving there on May 23, she led the troops out through the city gates of Compiegne for a nighttime attack.

Joan's attempt to relieve the siege of Compiegne failed, and the troops retreated back through the city gates. The governor, Guillaume de Flavy, ordered the drawbridge raised and the gates closed before all of them were safely inside. There is reason to believe that Flavy intentionally left Joan and some of the soldiers outside rather than jeopardize his entire garrison. Joan, her brother, her squire D'Aulon, and one of her chief lieutenants, Jean Poton de Xaintrailles, were captured. Joan wore a golden surcoat with long panels, and an archer in the service of the Bastard of Wandomme was able to grab hold of one of them and pull her off her horse.

The rules of chivalry required the archer to turn Joan over to Wandomme and for Wandomme to turn her over to his feudal overlord, John of Luxembourg, who was allied with the Burgundians. She remained in the custody of the Duke of Burgundy, held in a high tower cell in Luxembourg's castle at Beaurevoir, for six months, during which King Charles made no attempt to negotiate her release. Joan was essentially abandoned by the king who only held the throne because of her. Her entire ecclesiastical trial would be manipulated by the English and Burgundians to call into question the legitimacy of Charles' ascension to the French throne. At the same time, King Charles had become resentful of Joan's fame, which threatened to eclipse his own. He couldn't stand the idea that many of his own countrymen believed that he only ruled because Joan had put him on the throne. He used her as his own political pawn, knowing that if he simply stood back and let events unfold, he would rid himself of a major source of irritation.

Joan's Escape Attempt

The day after Joan was captured, on May 25, 1430, members of the theology faculty at the University of Paris wrote a letter to the Duke of Burgundy asking him to order John of

Luxembourg to hand over Joan for trial in an ecclesiastical court. This was the same group of theologians that would, the following year, assess the evidence gathered during a formal trial of the Inquisition. The Burgundians and the English could not have justifiably prosecuted Joan for having defeated them militarily, so they chose to let the Church do it for them.

After several long months of imprisonment in the tower of Luxembourg's castle, Joan attempted to escape by leaping from a window. She landed on soft ground and was not badly injured. but her daring escape attempt became a point of contention during her trial. She was grilled to determine whether her dangerous leap was a suicide attempt. She maintained that it was not because as she leaped, she had commended herself to God. She said that the Burgundians had already sold her to the English and that she would rather surrender her soul to God than fall into their hands. The Burgundians indeed handed Joan over to the English for a price of 10,000 livres, one livre being the equivalent of one pound of silver. It was rumored that John of Luxembourg actually sold Joan to the English over the protests of his own mother, wife, and daughter, all of whom approved of Joan and her mission. In December of that same year she was transferred to Rouen, the French military headquarters and administrative capital of King Henry VI of England.

Joan Is Delivered to English-Held Rouen for Trial

During the trial of rehabilitation twenty-five years after Joan's martyrdom, testimony was given about John of Luxembourg delivering Joan to the English in Rouen. The men accompanying him on the trip were some of the most powerful among the English in France. It was reported that John of Luxembourg offered to ransom Joan if she would agree not to fight the Burgundians any longer. If this event ever took place, it would have been an uncharacteristic act of chivalry on her captor's part—one that Joan rejected anyway, saying that nothing could make her give up her fight against the English invaders and their Burgundian allies. To the English and Burgundians, Joan was a challenge to the legitimacy of their regime, which they could not tolerate. In the centuries since her death at the stake, Joan of Arc has often been referred to as a "political pawn," one whose fate was predetermined before her trial even began. Many have compared her ordeal to that of Jesus, "destined to die on fabricated charges of religious impropriety."

Joan was tried in Rouen, an English stronghold and the capital of English Normandy, in an ecclesiastical court under the auspices of Pierre Cauchon, a staunch supporter of the English, who thought that their influence would help him become archbishop of Rouen. In fact, Cauchon truly hated the French and had no regard whatsoever for King Charles. Ruthlessly ambitious, he didn't even pretend to be open-minded about Joan's guilt or innocence, and he hand-picked like-minded lawyers and theologians as the other judges for his Court of the Inquisition. Joan's request for an equal number of French ecclesiastics was denied, although it was required under Canon law.

Cauchon flagrantly ignored court rules and laws during both the "preparatory" trial, which consisted of public interrogations and private ones held in Joan's prison cell for purposes of drawing up the articles with which Joan would be charged, and the subsequent "ordinary" trial on select articles, or charges. For example, there was a law that required all people under the age of 25 who were accused of heresy to be represented by a lawyer. Joan was denied legal counsel and had to defend herself against a rigged jury who were all aligned with the English. Paid by the English and all too willing to live up to the expectation that they would find Joan guilty, they clearly had a political agenda. Even the vice-inquisitor for Rouen, Jean Le Maistre, was uncomfortable with the blatant bias of Joan's trial and refused to be present for it, though his physical presence was required by Canon law. Without Le Maistre's presence and participation, the procedures would be deemed invalid. He only cooperated after the English threatened his life.

Meanwhile, Cauchon asked deliberately misleading questions designed to trap Joan in numerous "Catch 22," damned-if-you-do, damned-if-you-don't situations. He controlled access to the trial records and apparently deleted sections that were too sympathetic to Joan. On May 29, 1431, the judges, after hearing Cauchon's edited report, condemned Joan as a relapsed heretic and delivered her to the English to be burned at the stake.

While it's true that the particulars of Joan's trial were manipulated to ensure her condemnation, regarding her as a mere pawn undercuts the significance of her sacrifice. Pawns don't voluntarily sacrifice everything as a matter of faith and principle. Joan knew that she was being lured into cunning verbal traps designed to get her to seal her own fate. She may have been unlettered and theologically unsophisticated, but she was no fool.

Chapter 7: Joan's Prophecies

While Joan of Arc is known worldwide for her obedience to her voices, which she viewed as direct communications from God, she is not recognized by many today for her prophecies. Nor is it widely known that her own mission and role were believed by many in her time to be the embodiment of an earlier prophecy. Some attribute that earlier prophecy to the legendary Merlin, but others believe it originated with St. Bede the Venerable.

Was Joan the Prophesied Virgin Warrior?

For some years prior to Joan's birth, prophetic literature foretold that France would be delivered by a virgin. The stories were vague, but two details were consistently repeated and lent credence to Joan being the savior in question. The prophesied savior of France was always described as a young maid, specifically a young maid "from the borders of Lorraine," and Joan, who zealously guarded her maidenhood, came from a village near the border between France and the Duchy of Lorraine. These similarities predisposed the French to believe that Joan was the maiden in question and that she was on a divine mission for the salvation of France.

Some members of the dauphin's court took advantage of the widespread knowledge of these prophecies to promote Joan as the instrument of France's deliverance, as a way of garnering more support for Charles's claim to the throne. While being examined by the theologians at Poitier, Joan was reportedly questioned about a recent prophecy of an "armed woman who was to save the Kingdom." And testimony from Joan's uncle, Durand Laxart, who escorted Joan to Vaucouleurs both times that she went there seeking support for her mission from Robert de Baudricourt, suggested that Joan was well aware of the prophesies and used them to bolster belief in her mission. At Joan's rehabilitation trial, Laxart testified that she had told him "Was it not said that France would be ruined through a woman and afterwards restored by a virgin?" His account was corroborated by the woman with whom Joan had lodged during her second stay in Vaucouleurs.

During the fifth session of her preparatory trial, on March 1, 1431, Joan was questioned about certain letters she had dictated. During this exchange, she prophesied that "before seven years are past the English ... will lose everything in France." When asked how she knew this, she said that it had come to her by revelation.

During the seventh session, conducted privately in her cell with only a few assessors present, Joan was asked whether her voices played a role in her final battle, when she was captured by the Burgundians outside the walls of Compiegne. She said that she had been told by her voices that she would be captured before St. John's Day" and that "it had to be so." The question was not whether this and Joan's other visions and revelations were real, but whether they were of divine or satanic origin.

Yolande of Aragon, mother-in-law of Charles, was a known believer in visionaries and encouraged the idea that Joan was a mystic with prophetic visions. By the time of Charles's coronation in Reims, Joan had gained a reputation among the French as a prophetess and visionary.

Joan's Revelations

Here are the best-known prophesies made by Joan of Arc:

1. Joan would raise the siege of Orléans, which had been going on for seven months before she led the capture of the fortress of St. Loup on the first day of the battle for Orléans. This victory was followed by French victories over the English at the Fortress of the Augustines and

the stronghold of Les Tourelles, breaking the siege and realizing the prophecy.

2. Joan would be wounded during the battle for Les Tourelles. On the evening before, Joan asked her chaplain to stay close to her the next day and prophesied that "tomorrow blood will flow from my body, above my breast." During the attack on the fortress, while helping raise a ladder against a wall, Joan was indeed wounded by a crossbow bolt that struck her between the shoulder and her breast. The chaplain testified to these events during Joan's trial of rehabilitation. Joan herself was asked during her trial if she had really known beforehand that she would be injured. She answered in the affirmative and that she had told the king about it.

3. Joan would bring the dauphin to be crowned and anointed as Charles VII in the cathedral at Reims. She told Charles in March of 1429 that he would be crowned in four months, and he was, in fact, crowned in the Reims cathedral four months later, on July 17, 1429.

4. Joan would rescue the Duke of Orléans from the English, who had been holding him in captivity since the French defeat at Agincourt in 1415. Joan laid the groundwork by lifting the siege of Orléans, but he was not released until nine years after Joan's martyrdom.

5. Joan would drive all of the English out of France. Joan's prophecy that she would be the one to drive out the English may not have come true, but during her trial, she prophesied that within seven years, they would lose everything they held in France. The date that historians recognize as the point when the English were driven out of France is November 12, 1437, six years and eight months after Joan's prophesy.

There were several earlier examples of Joan's prophetic abilities. During her second trip to Vaucouleurs, Joan managed to convince Robert de Baudricourt to give her the resources to go to Chinon to meet with the dauphin by telling him that the French would suffer a major defeat near Orléans. Several days later, news of the French defeat reached Vaucouleurs, impressing Baudricout with Joan's prescience enough to send her on to Chinon. When Joan reached the dauphin in Chinon,

Charles announced to his court that Baudricourt had sent a girl claiming to be the Maid of Lorraine, the prophesied savior of France. As a test, Charles had a courtier sit on the throne while he disguised himself and mingled with the other courtiers. If Joan could identify him, he would acknowledge that she was divinely inspired. She did so without hesitation.

Witchcraft or Divine Inspiration?

Several other examples of Joan's prophetic abilities were brought up during her trial by her inquisitors in an attempt to paint certain incidents as evidence of witchcraft rather than divine inspiration. One of these regarded Joan's claim that she had received divine information from her voices about the location of a sword. When she sent someone to retrieve the sword from the church of St. Catherine de Fierbois, it was found where she said it would be and matched her description. One incident was used by the inquisitors as the basis for claiming that she caused a man's death through her words alone. The English commander taunted her from the ramparts of the fortress at Les Tourelles, yelling down to her "Milkmaid! Harlot!" Joan's response to him was "You insult me, but you are not far from your death." Soon after, he fell from the burning drawbridge into the Loire, was dragged under by his heavy armor, and drowned.

One of the events of which Joan apparently had foreknowledge was her own capture. When she prophesied to the dauphin in March of 1429 that he would be crowned within four months, she also said, "I shall last a year, and but little longer." She later told him that she would be captured by June 24, or Midsummer's Day, 1430. On May 23, the day she would lead an attack against the English besieging Compiègne, she prayed in a church and asked some children to pray for her because she had been betrayed. A few hours later, the governor of Compiègne raised the drawbridge and closed the city gates while Joan and some of her troops were still outside, and Joan was taken prisoner.

Joan's prophesies came to her by revelation, the source being her voices. Whether those voices were truly the voices of saints sent to her by God or the voices of demons, as alleged by Joan's inquisitors, was a central issue in her trial.

Chapter 8: Joan's Cross-Dressing

It's difficult for people living in the twenty-first century to understand the furor over Joan of Arc's decision to wear male clothing. Today, a woman who wears male clothing is making a fashion statement, or at most a lifestyle choice. But in fifteenth-century France, it was far more than that.

Joan First Adopts Men's Clothing

As far as we know, Joan donned male clothing for the first time for her trip from Vaucouleurs to Chinon after she convinced Robert de Beaudricourt, commander of the French troops, to give her the resources to travel to Chinon to offer her services to the Dauphin Charles. Two of the soldiers assigned to escort her on the dangerous journey through Burgundian territory suggested that she don male clothing to make her less conspicuous. Joan embraced the idea as a way to disguise her femininity and help protect her from sexual assault, as she had vowed to remain a virgin. Surrounded by men on a daily basis, Joan quickly made it her custom to wear only men's clothing.

Bishop Cauchon seized upon Joan's preference for wearing male clothing as wicked and unnatural and made it one of the key issues in her trial. She was charged with violating divine

law by dressing as a male and bearing arms. The specific
charge was defying the Deuteronomy 22:5: "The woman shall
not wear that which pertaineth unto a man, neither shall a
man put on a woman's garment: for all that do so are
abomination unto the Lord thy God." When summoned by
Cauchon for her first appearance before the ecclesiastical
court, Joan asked through the priest serving as bailiff
overseeing her incarceration that she be allowed to hear Mass.
The prosecutor, Jean d'Estivet, refused her request, citing as
the reason (according to the trial transcript) "the impropriety
of the garments to which she clung."

A Bargaining Chip

Throughout the preparatory trial (Joan's public and prison
interrogations), as the tribunal was finding it increasingly
difficult to come up with valid charges against her, Joan was
questioned repeatedly about her reasons for wearing men's
clothing. A number of promises were conditioned upon her
acceptance of woman's dress. At the close of the third session,
on February 24, 1431, Joan was asked if she would agree to
wear women's clothing if it were provided. Her reply was:
"Give me [a dress] and I will take it and go; otherwise, I am
content with this [her soldier's garb], since it pleases God that

I wear it." When the subject of her clothing came up again, during the sixth session, she was asked whether she adopted soldier's wear "by revelation." She explained that she had adopted it as protection while traveling behind enemy lines on her journey from Vaucouleurs to Chinon. She was asked about her male attire several other times during the session but refused to answer. When she was reminded that she had been offered women's clothing and had been asked to wear it in place of her soldier's clothing, she said that she "would not put it [her soldier's attire] off without God's leave."

When asked again during the ninth session of her trial why she wore male clothing, she stated that she chose to do so "of her own accord, and not at the request of any man alive." Pursuing the same line of questioning, she was asked if her voices had told her to dress as a soldier, to which she responded, "Everything I have done I have done at the instruction of my voices."

During the thirteenth session, on March 15, Joan asked once more to be allowed to hear Mass. Her inquisitors asked her whether it would be proper for her to hear Mass wearing men's clothing. Joan said, "Promise me that I'll get to hear Mass if I wear women' clothing." The interrogator made that promise. According to the trial transcript, Joan then replied: "And what do you say if I've promised our king and sworn not to remove these clothes? Nonetheless, I say, make me a long robe that touches the ground, with no train and give it to me for Mass. Then when I come back I'll put back on these clothes I'm wearing [her soldier's garb]."

A Central Concern in Joan's Ordinary Trial

After the fifteenth session of courtroom interrogation by her inquisitors, Joan's preparatory trial moved into the "ordinary" trial phase on March 26. During this phase, a list of seventy articles was drawn up (summarized later in a twelve-article indictment). The articles were read aloud in court, and Joan was questioned about each. Refusing to answer a charge had the same effect as admitting to it. On May 24, the ordinary trial ended with the abjuration—an opportunity for the condemned to renounce their previous behavior and beliefs in exchange for a lighter sentence.

It was apparently known that Joan was terrified of fire, which gave the inquisitors a way to pressure Joan into recanting. She was taken to see the stake prepared for her burning on the outskirts of Rouen and was told that she would be burned right away unless she signed an admission of guilt, renounced her voices, and stopped dressing as a soldier. She agreed and was taken back to her cell. Four days later, she recanted her abjuration and put on male clothing again, which was seen as a relapse into heresy.

When Cauchon and seven judges came to her cell to question her one last time, Joan was wearing a soldier's outfit that featured a tunic, hosen, and waist-high boots, all of which were fastened together with cords. Witnesses later said that it had been her custom throughout her incarceration to keep the cords tied together tightly as protection against being raped by the guards. A court scribe recalled that "she was then dressed in male clothing and was complaining that she could not give it up, fearing lest in the night her guards would inflict some act of outrage upon her; and she had complained once or twice to the Bishop of Beauvais, the Vice-Inquisitor, and Master Nicholas Loiseleur that one of the aforesaid guards had tried to rape her."

The transcript of this last interrogation shows that Joan was asked, "When, and why, did you revert to dressing as a man?" She responded, "I have done this on my own free will. Nobody has forced me; I prefer the apparel of a man to that of a woman." When asked "Why have you done this," she said, "It is both more seemly and proper to dress like this when surrounded by men, than wearing a woman's clothes. While I have been in prison, the English have molested me when I was dressed as a woman. I have done this to defend my modesty." Though there is no mention of it in the transcripts, the chief trial notary later reported that Joan had said that the judges promised to move her to a Church prison and follow the normal practice of assigning a nun to stay with her—and that Joan would wear only female clothing under those circumstances. That promise was not kept.

It seems likely that details such as these, that would reveal the lengths to which Cauchon was willing to go to convict Joan, may have been deliberately left out of the trial transcripts. Based on the later recollections of the trial bailiff, Jean Massieu, it is also likely that Joan was manipulated into reverting to male attire after her abjuration. Massieu's recollection was:

"When she had to get out of bed … she had requested of these Englishmen, her guards: 'Unchain me, so I can get up'. And then one of these Englishmen took away the female clothing which she had, and they emptied the sack in which the male clothing was, and tossed this clothing upon her while telling her, 'Get up'; and they put away the female clothing in the aforementioned sack. And, as she said, she put on the male clothing they had given her, saying, 'Sirs, you know this is forbidden me: without fail, I will not accept it.' But nevertheless they wouldn't give her anything else, so that she continued in this argument with them until the hour of noon; and finally, she was compelled by the necessity of the body to leave the room and hence to wear this clothing; and after she returned, they still wouldn't give her anything else [to wear] regardless of any appeal or request she made of them."

In addition to reverting to male clothing, Joan told Cauchon and the seven judges that she had heard her voices again. Cauchon concluded that her voices were really the voice of the devil, convincing her to dress like a man again, and declared her a relapsed heretic, which condemned Joan to burn at the stake.

It's true that in the fifteenth century, cross-dressing was considered sinful by the Church, but prior to Joan's martyrdom, there's no evidence that anyone was ever prosecuted for it, let alone condemned to die. Even St. Thomas Aquinas, who was born about two hundred years before Joan, wrote that there might be occasions when, although it was sinful, women might be excused for wearing male attire "on account of some necessity, either in order to hide oneself from enemies, or through lack of other clothes, or for some similar motive." Cauchon would have known this, which is why it was imperative to arrive at the official conclusion that Joan was counseled by the devil to dress like a man. Joan wasn't executed simply for cross-dressing, but because the devil allegedly made her do it.

Chapter 9: Joan's Preparatory Trial— The Public Sessions

It has been said that the trial of Joan of Arc was second in importance only to the trial of Jesus Christ, but far more is known about Joan's. Every minute of Joan's trial was recorded in real time, in the minutes written in French by Guillaume Manchon, the trial notary. Those minutes were later translated into Latin by Manchon and one of the judges, Thomas de Courcelles, most likely around 1435. The trial record also included all of the official letters written during and about the trial by Pierre Cauchon, chief inquisitor and bishop of Beauvais; the vice inquisitor, Jean Le Maistre; and the theologians of the faculty of the University of Paris. Five handwritten copies were made, three of which still exist today. Manchon's original notes written in French have been lost. The entire trial record was not completely translated into English until 1932.

Considering who and what Joan was up against throughout her trial, her conviction was a virtual certainty from the very beginning. Most of the sixty judges were affiliated with the University of Paris, and many of them had close ties to the English. Some had even been on the English payroll at one time or another. All of them were trained in the law and academic rhetoric, and most of them were her avowed enemies. Many of them had suffered in one way or another as the result of Joan's victories, having been driven out of the dioceses from which they derived their power and revenues.

The circumstances under which Joan was imprisoned for the duration of her trial weakened her physically, though she remained resolute in defending herself and her mission. She should rightly have been in the ecclesiastical prison, as hers was an ecclesiastical trial, not a secular one. In an ecclesiastical prison, she would have been guarded and attended by women, but in her cell in the castle of Rouen, an English stronghold, she was kept in chains and guarded by men, who taunted and abused her.

The sixty learned and accomplished men summoned to try Joan knew what was expected of them. They knew that "dynasties trembled in the balance." But they also knew what Joan, an uneducated teenaged girl, had accomplished, and recognized that the King of Heaven has often used the most unlikely individuals, the humblest of vessels, to do his work. They believed that God speaks through his saints and knew that Joan had prophesied events that had, in fact, come to pass. They knew that though Joan's enemies painted her as a harlot, Joan had been examined by respectable and honest women, most recently by the Duchess of Bedford and her ladies, and had been found to be a virgin. They knew that Cauchon's superior, the Archbishop of Reims, had led the ecclesiastical examination of Joan at Poitiers and had found her to be a good and virtuous Catholic. And they knew that Le Maistre, appointed as vice inquisitor for Joan's trial, opposed the proceedings. One can imagine these men having to weigh their beliefs and values and the evidence against the expectations of their religious and secular superiors—for a swift guilty verdict that would allow Joan to be handed over to secular authorities for execution of her sentence.

Medieval ecclesiastical trials followed a prescribed structure and sequence of events, and Joan's was no exception.

January 9, 1431. The First Day of the Proceedings

Bishop Cauchon opened the proceedings by describing the summons of the judges and reading into the record several letters, including:

- The letter from the University of Paris to the Duke of Burgundy, demanding that Joan be handed over to the inquisitor of the faith, or be surrendered to Cauchon for trial.

- The letter from the University of Paris to John of Luxembourg, reminding him that his duty to the Church superseded his duty to the state and demanding that Joan be turned over to the Inquisitor of the Faith or to Bishop Cauchon.

- The letter from the vicar-general, the inquisitor of the faith, to the Duke of Burgundy, demanding that Joan be surrendered to appear before the procurator of the Inquisition.

- The summons from Couchon to the Duke of Burgundy, John of Luxembourg, and the Bastard of Wandomme, demanding that Joan be "sent to the King to be delivered to the Church" (i.e., to Cauchon) for trial and offering a reward for those who captured and held her.

- Letters from the University of Paris to Cauchon, chiding him for not having been more aggressive in demanding the surrender of Joan for trial before an ecclesiastical court and urging him to have her brought to Paris "so that the trial may be diligently examined and competently conducted."

- The letter from the University of Paris to the English king, bemoaning the long wait for the surrender of Joan and urging the king to command that she be "delivered into the hands of the justice of the Church [Beauvais] and to the Inquisitor of France" for determination of the charges against her. This and previous letters implied that only in Paris could the job be done well.

- The letter from the king of England to Cauchon upon the delivery of Joan to him in Rouen (rather than to the University of Paris). The king clearly stated his intention to "retake and regain possession" of Joan if Cauchon failed to secure a conviction.

- A number of letters of a procedural nature, granting Cauchon the right to occupy the cathedral at Rouen in the absence of an archbishop and appointing a promotor general or procurator (Jean d'Estivet), counselors, notaries, and scribes.

January 13, 1431. Reading of the Evidence Against Joan

Cauchon assembled a group of theologians to examine evidence and draw up articles against Joan. They spent three days working on the articles.

January 23, 1431. Decision Concerning the Preparatory Information

Cauchon met with certain theologians to review the articles that had been drawn up and determine the next steps. The decision was to draw up the preparatory information based on Joan's acts and declarations to determine if there was sufficient cause to proceed against her. An expert in canon law, Jean de La Fontaine, was appointed to this task.

February 13, 1431. The Officers Appointed Take Oath

The people appointed as judges and to play other roles in Joan's trial appeared before Cauchon and took an oath to fulfill and exercise their offices faithfully.

February 14–16, 1431. The Preparatory Information Is Drawn Up

After taking the oath, Jean de La Fontaine, assisted by two notaries, spent the next four days compiling the preparatory information that had been gathered.

February 19, 1431. Decision to Summon the Inquisitor

A group of "lords and masters" was assembled by Cauchon to read the articles and depositions included in the preparatory evidence. Not surprisingly, they concluded that there was sufficient evidence to proceed with the trial and call Joan to "reply to certain interrogations to be addressed to her." On the advice of experienced theologians in the group, Cauchon decided to summon the Lord Inquisitor of Heretical Error for the Kingdom of France to participate in the trial. In his absence from the city, his deputy, Jean Le Maistre, the vicar of the Lord Inquisitor, was summoned in his place that very day. A few hours later, Le Maistre appeared before Cauchon and said that while he would "gladly perform all that he was in duty bound to do on behalf of the holy inquisition," he did not think his commission, which applied only to the diocese and city of Rouen, would allow him to participate in the trial, which was under the jurisdiction of Cauchon as bishop of Beauvais. This was the first indication that Le Maistre was going to be a reluctant participant in the trial.

Tuesday, February 20, 1431. The Vicar of the Lord Inquisitor Refuses to Act

The next day, Jean Le Maistre; Nicolas Loiseleur, canon of the cathedral of Rouen; Brother Martin Ladvenu of the Order of

Preaching Brothers, to which Le Maistre belonged; and several others visited Cauchon in his residence and were told that the experts Cauchon had consulted had determined that Le Maistre's commission did allow him to participate in the trial. However, Cauchon had decided to send a summons to the Lord Inquisitor, requesting that he return to Rouen and conduct the trial himself or delegate that responsibility to Le Maistre or another deputy. Le Maistre stated that he would not take part in conducting the trial unless he were given special authority beyond his current commission, and he urged Cauchon to proceed without him until he received more counsel about whether his commission permitted him to participate. Le Maistre specifically noted that he was taking that stance "for the serenity of his conscience and the safer conduct of the trial." Cauchon issued a summons for Joan to appear before the court on Wednesday, February 29.

Wednesday, February 21, 1431. The First Public Session

Cauchon convened the first public session of the tribunal at eight o'clock in the morning with a number of "reverend fathers, lords, and masters" present. Letters of citation and writ from the king of England were read aloud, and the decision to deny Joan's request to be allowed to hear Mass was announced. Joan was led into the presence of the tribunal, where Cauchon provided an explanation as to why she had been summoned to answer "interrogations in matters of faith." He required Joan to take an oath with her hands on the holy gospels.

Joan balked at taking the oath because she might be asked things that she would not tell. She did agree that she would gladly swear to answer truthfully questions about her parents and what she had done since leaving their home, but she had never told anyone other than King Charles about her revelations from God and would not reveal them to save her life. She was repeatedly admonished to take an oath to speak the truth in matters of faith. Joan knelt, placed both hands upon the missal, and swore to answer truthfully whatever should be asked her concerning matters of faith, but remained silent as to not telling anyone about the divine revelations made to her.

Joan was then questioned about her parentage and place of birth, her baptism and the identity of her godparents, her age, and her religious education. She repeatedly refused to say the Paternoster to demonstrate her knowledge unless she could do so in confession. Cauchon warned her against attempting to escape, and when she complained about being kept in iron chains, he reminded her of her attempt to leap from the window of her tower cell in the castle of John of Luxembourg. John Grey, squire to the bodyguard of the king of England, was appointed, along with Jean Berwoit and William Talbot, to guard her and prevent anyone from speaking to her without Cauchon's permission. Joan was ordered to appear at the same time the next morning.

Thursday, February 22, 1431. Second Session

The second session began with Cauchon informing the assembly of Le Maistre's presence as a stand-in for the absent Lord Inquisitor and of his initial concerns about participating. Le Maistre concurred with Couchon's recitation of the facts and stated that he was content that the trial continue. When Joan was brought in, she was once again required to take an oath, but she protested that the one she had taken the previous day should suffice. Eventually, she swore to tell the truth about matters of faith.

Master Jean Beaupère, professor of sacred theology, began the questioning by asking Joan about her childhood—specifically, how old he was when she left her father's house (she could not vouch for her age), whether she had learned any craft (yes, in sewing and spinning, she feared no woman in Rouen), what her responsibilities were as a youth (ordinary domestic chores), how often she confessed (once a year) and received the sacrament of the Eucharist (at Easter). She declined to say whether she ever received the sacrament of the Eucharist at any other feasts, and then added that when she was thirteen, a voice from God began to "help and guide" her.

Joan testified that although she was afraid when she first heard the voice, she believed it was sent from God, and when she heard it the third time, she knew that it was the voice of an angel. She said that she heard the voice more frequently after arriving in France, that it always protected her, and that she always understood it. The voice was almost always accompanied by a bright light.

Beaupère pressed Joan about the form in which the voice appeared to her, but she told him he would not learn that from her. He also wanted to know what the voice told her. She said that at first it simply told her to be good and go to church often, and then it told her, at least once or twice a week, to go to France. Then, she said, it told her that she should raise the siege of Orleans. She added that the voice told her to go to

Robert de Baudricourt in Vaucouleur and he would help her. She said that she protested at first, because she was a young maid who knew nothing about riding or fighting. She told the judges about traveling to Vaucouleur with her uncle and that her voice enabled her to recognize Baudricourt despite never having seen him before. The voice also told her what to expect, so Joan was persistent when Baudricourt refused twice to hear her. She recounted that he listened to her the third time she appealed to him for help to get to France to see the dauphin.

Joan testified about leaving Vaucouleurs while wearing a man's clothing and carrying a sword, in the company of a knight, a squire, and four servants provided by Robert de Baudricourt. She described her journey and frequently hearing the voices. She was asked several times why she started wearing male attire, at which she either refused to answer or gave vague and conflicting responses.

When asked about the letter she sent to the English surrounding Orleans, she noted several alterations that had been made to the copy read to her in Rouen. Most notable was the substitution of "Surrender to the Maid," for what she had written: "Surrender to the King."

Joan continued her recitation of events by describing her trip to Chinon to see the dauphin, to whom she always referred as "the king." She credited her voice for identifying the king for her, just as it had enabled her to recognize Baudricourt. She refused to answer when asked if the voice was accompanied by a light or if she saw an angel above the king. She did say that before the king sent her out with the troops, he experienced several apparitions and revelations, but when asked to describe them, she said, "Send to the king and he will tell you." She said that members of her party knew that her voice was sent by God and that her king and others heard and saw the voices. Moreover, she said that she heard the voice daily and needed it, but she denied ever asking it for any final reward other than the salvation of her soul.

Toward the end of the session, Joan confessed that she had attempted an assault on Paris. When asked if that happened on a feast day, she said that she thought it had, but she refused to answer the follow-up question as to whether that was a good thing to do.

February 24, 1431. Third Session

The third session began with Joan once again protesting the taking of the oath, saying, "You may well do without it! I have sworn enough, twice." Cauchon persisted in demanding that she swear, and Joan persisted in saying that she would gladly tell some of what she knew, but not all. She finally agreed to tell the truth in matters concerning the trial, after which Jean Beaupère continued the questioning. His focus was on when Joan had last heard the voice, what the circumstances were, whether the voice was accompanied by a great light, what she saw, and what the voice had told her. He was particularly interested in any physical manifestation and what Joan believed the origin of the voice to be. Joan said that she had been awakened by the voice the day before and heard it two more times that day. She reported that she had asked the voice for counsel and was advised to answer her interrogators boldly, for God would comfort her. She then warned Cauchon that he was putting himself in great peril because she was sent by God. When pressed as to whether the voice had forbidden her to answer any questions, she replied, "Believe me, it was not men who forbade me." And she continued to profess her firm belief in the Christian faith and that the voice came to her from God.

It was during this third session that Joan offered a response often cited as evidence of her amazing ability, as an unschooled teenager, to keep from falling into traps set for her by her interrogators. She was asked whether she knew if she was in God's grace, and she was smart enough to know that either a "yes" or "no" response could be used against her. Therefore, she answered: "If I am not, may God put me there; and if I am, may God so keep me. I should be the saddest creature in the world if I knew I were not in His grace."

When the questioning turned to the subject of her opinions of the Burgundians, she was not quite as circumspect. She said that she only knew one Burgundian and would have been "quite willing for him to have his head cut off if it had pleased God." She responded to questions as to whether the voice told her to hate the Burgundians by saying that since the voice was for the king of France, she did not like the Burgundians.

Before the session ended, the interrogators were clearly fishing for evidence to support the charge of witchcraft. The questions focused on a tree growing near Domrémy that was called the Ladies Tree or the Fairies' Tree and a nearby fountain from which the sick drank when they sought to be cured of their illnesses. Joan spoke of joining other village girls in playing near the tree and making garlands there for Our Lady of Domrémy. She explained that while she had heard old folks tell tales about fairies frequenting the tree, she had no reason to believe the stories and denied ever seeing any fairies or knowing anyone who said they had. Similarly, she said she had heard of sick people drinking from the fountain but did not know whether they were cured.

Tuesday, February 27, 1431. Fourth Session

After what was becoming Joan's standard protest over taking an oath, Jean Beaupère began the questioning by asking whether Joan had been fasting for Lent. It was in response to one of Beaupère's questions that Joan first named the saints who were speaking to her—St. Catherine, St. Margaret, and St. Michael—and described them as wearing beautiful crowns. She also said that she had God's permission to reveal their identities, as she had done during her examination at Poitiers. Numerous questions followed regarding the saints' physical appearance, their manner of speech, and whether they spoke to her separately or together. She said that St. Michael spoke to her first, when she was about 13, and that she saw him and the many angels who accompanied him. When asked if she saw them bodily and corporeally, she said, "I saw them with my bodily eyes as well as I see you; and when they left me, I wept; and I fain would have had them take me with them too." Joan referred repeatedly to her testimony before the commission at Poitiers and refused to answer further any questions that she said she had not received God's permission to answer. On the subject of wearing male attire, she said she did so at the command of God and the angels.

The other main areas of inquiry during the session included what revelations the king had experienced that made him believe in her mission; the rusty sword that was found in the church of St. Catherine de Fierbois, exactly where Joan's voices had told her it would be; and Joan's prophesy that she would be wounded during the assault on the fortress on the bridge outside of Orleans.

March 4–9, 1431. End of the Public Sessions

The fifth and sixth public sessions continued with the interrogators focusing relentlessly on the same subjects: the physical manifestations of Joan's voices, her prophecies and revelations, her knowledge of witchcraft (such as the use of the mandrake root), her preference for male attire, rumors that people had come to her seeking healing, and her religious beliefs and practices. At the end of the sixth session, Cauchon declared that all of the information obtained from Joan so far would be examined by certain experts in canon and civil law to determine if there were further points on which Joan should be examined at further length. These experts spent several days reviewing the notaries' minutes and then gathered in Cauchon's residence. The outcome of that meeting was a list of points for further examination and the appointment of Jean de La Fontaine to continue the interrogation of Joan in her prison cell.

Chapter 10: Joan's Trial—The Prison Sessions

Saturday, March 10, 1431. First Session in Prison

Jean de La Fontaine, Cauchon's deputy, conducted the interrogations that took place in Joan's cell, in the presence of two doctors of theology, an expert in the law, and the priest Jean Massieu. His first line of questioning focused on the events leading up to Joan's capture at Compiègne, from her arrival in the town early in the morning of her final day of freedom. She revealed that her capture had been foretold to her repeatedly by St. Catherine and St. Margaret. Though they did not tell her exactly when she would be taken prisoner, they told Joan that God would aid her. De La Fontaine also asked about the sign she gave the dauphin when she went to him. She would not describe it, but she said that many of those present saw and heard it, that it was with the king's treasure, and that it would last for a thousand years or more. Pressed on the matter, she said an angel from God had presented the sign to the king (she invariably referred to Charles as the king, even before his coronation) and added that more than three hundred people had reportedly seen the sign after she left the king's presence.

Monday, March 12, 1431. Second Session in Prison

The following Monday, March 12, Jean Le Maistre, vicar of the Lord Inquisitor of Heretical Error in the Kingdom of France, appeared in Cauchon's residence, where several lords and masters were gathered. He had been summoned by Cauchon to read the letter from the Lord Inquisitor appointing Le Maistre to serve in his stead for the duration of the trial. The prison interrogation continued that same morning. Jean de La Fontaine continued his questioning about the sign Joan said had been brought to Charles by an angel and about her interactions with that angel, as well as with St. Catherine and St. Margaret. Joan said that they never failed to appear when she needed them, even without her calling for them.

Of particular interest to de La Fontaine was the issue of Joan's virginity and why she had summoned a man from the town of Toul for breach of promise. Joan set the record straight, saying that it was the other way around. He had summoned her, though she had made no promise to him. If any promise of marriage had been made, it was by her parents. The promise she had made at age 13, to keep her virginity as long as it pleased God that she do so, prevented her from making promises to any man. The questioning continued through the afternoon, touching on many matters about which Joan had been interrogated during the public sessions, particularly her cross-dressing and her virginity. There was a concerted effort throughout the trial to portray her as a wanton woman.

Tuesday, March 13, 1431. Third Session in Prison

The next day, Jean Le Maistre joined the lords and masters gathered in Joan's cell. Joan was informed of his role and of the appointment of Jean d'Estivet as promoter or procurator general, who would henceforth conduct the trial. Joan was further questioned about the sign she gave Charles—the crown brought by an angel. She was asked whether the angel put the crown on the dauphin's head, how the angel entered and left the room, whether the angel spoke, what reverence she paid the angel, what the crown was made of, who was present at the time, and much more. Some of her answers were consistent with her earlier response, but some were not, and at several points she refused to respond. The session ended with questions about her attack on Paris.

Wednesday, March 14, 1431. Fourth Session in Prison

Wednesday's session focused on Joan's leap from the tower of the castle of John of Luxembourg, where she was held following her capture. The questions clearly were aimed at proving that Joan either had attempted suicide or had leapt believing God would save her. Joan denied that her voices had encouraged her leap and said that St. Catherine told her repeatedly not to jump. She said that she was simply hoping to escape and not be handed over to the English. Besides, she later confessed herself on the advice of St. Catherine, asking pardon of God for having risked her life foolishly, and St. Catherine assured her that she had been forgiven.

The questioning shifted to Joan's certainty of her salvation, and Joan explained that she believed she would be saved if she kept her promise to God to keep safe her virginity of body and soul. When asked if she needed to confess, she said that if she were in mortal sin, her saints would have abandoned her. Several other unsuccessful attempts were made to establish Joan as being in mortal sin, including accusing her of horse theft and of being responsible for the execution of a man who had confessed to murder, theft, and treason.

Thursday, March 15, 1431. Fifth Session in Prison

The interrogation started with more questions about Joan's leap from the tower of Luxembourg's castle against the wishes of her saints, followed by Joan being asked if she would attempt to escape from her current cell if she had the opportunity to do so. She said that if she saw the opportunity, she would assume that God was giving her permission to escape. Without that permission, she would only flee if she made a forcible attempt and was successful, as her success would prove that God was pleased with her and was giving her permission to go.

There was then more questioning about Joan's willingness to wear a dress if it meant she would be allowed to hear Mass. She refused to answer unless she was given a solemn promise that she would be permitted to hear Mass if she wore a dress. The examiner made that promise, but Joan said she would have to ask the saints to counsel her on the subject before accepting the offer. The focus then switched to questions about Joan's willingness to submit to the decision of the Church and whether she bowed down to her voices and lit candles to them as she would to a saint. She professed her obedience to St. Catherine, St. Margaret, and St. Michael. She said that she made no distinction between the saints in heaven and the saints who appeared to her, and that she always did her best to accomplish what the saints bade her to do because she knew they only asked her to do what Our Lord wanted her to do.

The examiner asked Joan how she knew that her voices were good spirits, and she responded by saying that they always guided and comforted her and that "St. Michael certified it before they came to me." Pressed on the subject, she said that at first, she had "grave doubts" about his identity and saw him a number of times before she knew he was St. Michael. The first time she saw him, she said, she was afraid, and she saw him many times before she knew he was St. Michael. Asked what convinced her, she said it was because he told her to go to the aid of the rightful king of France and that he would help her.

Saturday, March 17, 1431. Sixth Session in Prison

Once again, the examiners grilled Joan on the physical appearance of St. Michael, her willingness to submit to the judgment of the Church Militant (the Church on earth, comprising the pope, cardinals, prelates, clergy, and all good Catholics). Joan answered that her mission in France was at the command of the Church Triumphant (God, the saints, and all souls who are already saved). She gladly submitted all of her deeds to the Church Triumphant but said nothing about submission to the Church Militant. She further said that though she believed God would not let her be condemned, if it came to that, she requested a woman's dress and a hood for her head. The examiners found her response perplexing, given her ongoing refusal to wear a dress, and they asked her if it would please God if she agreed to wear a woman's dress if that meant she would be released. Joan said she would never agree not to wear men's clothing and take up a sword to do the Lord's will.

The interrogation continued to try to elicit damning answers from Joan about fairies, whether she believed that God and the saints hated England, the symbols and saints' images on her arms and pennant, whether the saints looked like their painted depictions, why only she carried the standard and whether the French would have been victorious if someone else had carried it, and whether she would have succeeded in battle or would have continued to hear her voices if she lost her virginity. There were some questions Joan would not answer, and the answers she did give were often vague or unrelated to the questions. There was a concerted effort to prove that the saints Joan heard and saw were not saints, but demons, and that Joan consorted with fairies and otherwise participated in witchcraft.

Passion Sunday, March 18, 1431. Presentation of Joan's Statements to the Assessors

Cauchon assembled the inquisitors and assessors and had many of Joan's statements read aloud. The assessors were charged with considering the evidence, consulting "authoritative books," and presenting their opinions the following Thursday. In the meantime, articles were to be drawn up to be brought against Joan in court before the judges. When they met again on Thursday, March 22, the list of articles was whittled down and reined.

Saturday, March 24, 1431. The Interrogations Are Read in Joan's Presence

The record of Joan's interrogations was read aloud to her in French, in her prison, by the notary Guillaume Manchon, in front of Cauchon, Jean de La Fontaine (the interrogator), Jean Le Maistre (vicar of the Lord Inquisitor), and several other "venerable lords and masters." The record was read from beginning to end, in sequence, after Joan agreed that anything she did not contradict during the reading would be considered "true and confessed."

Palm Sunday, March 26, 1431. Joan Asks Permission to Hear Mass

On the morning of Palm Sunday, Cauchon and a few legal experts visited Joan in her cell and told Jean that she would be allowed to hear Mass that day if she would put on a dress. Joan requested to be allowed to hear Mass in her male clothing and to receive the sacrament of the Eucharist on Easter Sunday. Cauchon refused to answer until she said whether she would wear a dress if they acceded to her request. Joan said that she could not agree because she had not received counsel on the matter. The men told Joan to ask her voices whether she could put on a dress to receive the Eucharist on Easter, but she clung to her earlier refusals to change her manner of dress and asked to be allowed to hear Mass in her male clothing, as "it did not burden her soul and … the wearing of it was not against the Church."

Chapter 11: The Ordinary Trial

March 26, 1431. Beginning of the Ordinary Trial

Cauchon met with Le Maistre and other court officials, lords, and master in his residence to read the final articles against Joan resulting from her preparatory trial, and the decision was made to proceed with the ordinary trial. Any articles that Joan refused to answer after being canonically admonished would be held to be confessed. On the following day, the court assembled and Joan was led in to hear the final articles against her read in French. She was first assured that the assessors' intent was not to seek vengeance or corporal punishment, but rather "her instruction and her return to the ways of truth and salvation." She was offered counsel, but Joan said she would take her counsel from Our Lord.

The reading of the seventy articles of accusation against Joan began with an acknowledgement of the authority of Cauchon, as ordinary judge, and Le Maistre, as inquisitor of the faith, to pass judgment on Joan. Though Joan acknowledged their role in protecting the Christian faith and the punishment of those who fall from it, she stated that she would submit only to "the Church in Heaven, that is to God, to the Blessed Virgin Mary and to the Saints of Paradise," and firmly believed that she had not failed in the faith.

Over the next few days, Joan listened to each of the articles and the evidence offered in support of them. Although she provided clarification on some points and referred often to the responses she had given to her interrogators, she denied all of the articles.

A "digest" of the articles of accusation was prepared, whittling the list of seventy articles down to twelve, and submitted to the assessors for deliberation. After examining the eleven written opinions that were returned, Cauchon decided "to exhort her charitably and gently admonish her, and to have her admonished gently by many men of honesty and learning, doctors and others, in order to lead her back to the way of truth and a sincere profession of the faith." Cauchon and seven others went to Joan in prison on Wednesday, April 18, to "charitably exhort" Joan to reconsider certain statements she had made that were considered dangerous from the point of view of the faith. As she was an "unlettered and ignorant woman," and they were "wise and learned men, upright and kindly," they would instruct her "for the salvation of her body and soul." But if she chose to trust "her own mind and inexperienced head," they would be "compelled to abandon her."

Joan was ill at the time of their visit and asked to receive the sacraments and be buried in holy ground should God decide to take her. Cauchon insisted that she submit to the Church Militant if she wanted to "enjoy the rights of the Church as a Catholic." Still, Joan refused to alter her testimony, saying, "Whatever happens to me I will do and say nothing except what I have already said in the trial." She said she was a good Christian and would die a good Christian.

Wednesday, May 2, 1431. Public Admonition

The judges, lords, and masters assembled in the great hall of the castle at Rouen and were addressed by Cauchon. He said that though the case had not yet been formally decided, Joan seemed "reprehensible in many points," yet the Court thought it fitting to "endeavor by every possible means to instruct this woman on the points in which she seems to be in error, and, as far as we are able, to bring her back to the way and knowledge of truth." Since none of the private efforts to do so had succeeded, perhaps being admonished by the gathered assembly would "more easily induce her to humility and obedience and dissuade her from too much reliance on her own opinion." Jean de Châtillon, archdeacon of Évreux, was chosen to deliver the admonition to Joan and "show her the way of the truth."

Joan was led onto the hall and advised by Cauchon to pay careful attention to the advice and warnings of de Châtillon, for if she didn't agree with what he would tell her for the salvation of her body and soul, the latter were in great peril. The archdeacon de Châtillon admonished Joan for the following errors:

- Refusing to submit to the authority of the Church Militant, which derives its authority from God and is empowered to "know and judge the deeds of the faithful, whether they were good or evil"

- Persisting in wearing man's dress, "in the fashion of men-at-arms ... which is scandalous and against good living and custom" and "contrary to the commandments of God declared in Deuteronomy"

- Attributing "the responsibility for her sins to God and his saints," which was blasphemous

- Having invented falsehoods about her revelations and apparitions and believing "audaciously that [she] is fit to receive them"

- Usurping the office of God by prophesying future events and presuming that she would be forgiven for leaping from the tower of the Luxembourgs, which was "nothing but divination, presumption, and rashness"

Joan responded to these admonitions in much the same way she had addressed the same subjects during her interrogations—referring the archdeacon and judges to the written record of her earlier questioning. Cauchon urged Joan to change her mind, and she asked, "How long will you give me to think it over?" He told her he needed an immediate answer. When she refused to reply, she was returned to her cell.

May 9, 1431. Joan Is Threatened with Torture

A week later, on May 9, Joan was brought before the judges and once again admonished to tell the truth about what they considered false replies. She was threatened with torture if she did not confess, and she was shown both the instruments of torture and the men who would wield them. Joan responded, "Truly, if you were to tear me limb from limb and separate my soul from my body, I would not tell you anything more: and if I did say anything, I should afterwards declare that you had compelled me to say it by force." She said that she had been comforted and counseled by St. Gabriel and her voices and that when she asked them if she would be burned, they said that "she must wait upon God, and He would aid her." The judges ultimately decided against torture, as they thought (with a few dissents) that "it would be of little profit to her." The actual opinions of the judges, as captured in the trial records, had more to do with their fear of a trial "so well conducted" being "exposed to calumny."

May, 19, 1431. The Deliberations of the University of Paris Are Read

On the following Saturday, May 19, the court gathered to consider the opinions received from faculty members of the University of Paris after they had been asked to review the twelve articles against Joan. The response from the University was presented in the form of a public instrument, which included a letter to the King of France and England. The letter expressed the faculty's approval of the way the trial was conducted and urged that it be brought to a swift conclusion.

The letter addressed to Cauchon exaggerated the danger Joan presented, saying that "her poison" had infected the "most Christian flock of almost the entire western world" and praised Cauchon's zeal in conducting the trial.

The faculty rendered an opinion on each of the twelve articles, declaring Joan's revelations to be "fictitious, pernicious and misleading lies, or ... superstitions, proceeding from evil or diabolical spirits, such as Belial, Satan and Behemoth." They described Joan's testimony about the sign the angels gave to the dauphin to be "a presumptuous, misleading, pernicious, feigned lie, hostile to the dignity of angels." They rejected Joan's identification of her voices as unfounded and determined her testimony about her prophecies to be "nothing but superstition, divination, presumptuous affirmation and vain boasting."

As to Joan dressing in soldier's garb, they called it "blasphemous and contemptuous of God." Her military actions were proof that Joan was "treacherous, cunning, cruel, athirst for the spilling of human blood, seditious, inciting to tyranny, and blasphemous of God in her commands and revelations." For leaving home without parental permission and seeking help from Robert de Beaudricourt, she was deemed "impious towards her parents, contemptuous of the commandment to honor her father and mother, scandalous [and] blasphemous toward God." Her attempted escape by leaping from a high tower was interpreted as a suicide attempt and exhibited "an erroneous opinion ... concerning man's free will." Her belief that the saints would conduct her to Paradise if she remained pure of body and soul was "a rash and presumptuous assertion, a pernicious falsehood" showing that Joan "holds evil opinions in matters of faith." Joan's claims to know by revelation that the saints were on the side of the English was seen as "superstitious divination, blasphemy of St. Catherine and St. Margaret, and transgression of the commandment to love her neighbor." Her relationship with her voices, characterized by revelations and apparitions, and her reverence for St. Michael, St. Catherine, and St. Margaret were proof of idolatry. And her refusal to submit to the Church Militant made her an apostate.

Wednesday, May 23, 1431. The Trial Is Concluded

On Wednesday, May 23, Joan was brought before the tribunal and several others to have her faults and crimes, as concluded by the faculty of the University of Paris, explained to her. She was given one last chance to admit to them and submit to the "correction and decision of our Holy Mother the Church." This was presented to her as a kindness, so that she might not be forever separated from Our Lord. She was admonished and exhorted to reform her ways and beliefs and submit to the Church Militant to save her soul, and perhaps her body, from death.

Joan replied, "As for my words and deeds, which I declared in the trial, I refer to them and will maintain them." She said that even if she saw the executioner "ready to kindle the fire, and she herself were in it, she would say nothing else and would maintain until death what she said in the trial."

The judges then declared the trial over and proclaimed that Joan's sentence would be pronounced and carried out the next day.

Chapter 12: Joan's Martyrdom and Rehabilitation

May 24, 1431. The Public Sermon

The trial transcript fails to mention that Joan's recantation occurred only after she had been taken out to see the stake set up on the outskirts of Rouen, with kindling and bundles of wood stacked around it. Nor is there any mention of Joan's longstanding terror of fire. The transcript only says that when the court gathered on the morning of May 24 in the cemetery of the Abbey of Saint-Ouen at Rouen, Joan was present, standing on a scaffold or platform. It does include a summary of the sermon delivered by Guillaume Erart, Doctor of Sacred Theology, for the "salutary admonition" of Joan and the many people assembled there. At the end of the sermon, the good doctor spoke directly to Joan. He urged Joan to submit to the Church and revoke "all her words and deeds" of which the clergy disapproved, but Joan said, "I refer me to God and to our Holy Father the Pope." She was told that this would not suffice, and Cauchon began to read the formal sentence.

Joan Recants

According to the trial transcript, Joan suddenly interrupted and said the she would submit to the Church, to all her judges decreed, and would obey their "ordinance and will in all

110

things." She then recanted and abjured by making an "X" on the written abjuration read to her in French. It admitted to everything of which she was accused and swore that she would never return to her errors. Cauchon then rescinded her earlier excommunication and sentenced her to life imprisonment. Later that afternoon, Cauchon, Le Maistre, and several others came to Joan's cell. She was told that she must henceforth wear a woman's dress, and she was given one, which she put on, and she allowed her head to be shaved.

May 28, 1431. Joan Relapses

Four days later, when Cauchon and the judges returned to Joan's cell, they found her wearing male attire. The only reasons she would give for resuming male dress was that she preferred it to woman's dress, she was surrounded by men, and the promises made to her about permitting her to hear Mass, receive the Eucharist, and remove her chains had not been kept. When asked if she had heard her voices since her abjuration, she said that she had, and that they brought word to her from God that she had damned herself to save her life. According to Joan, St. Catherine and St. Margaret told her she had "done a great evil in declaring that what she had done was wrong." Joan said that she didn't really understand the content of the abjuration and that she only recanted for fear of the fire.

Though the trial record transcript portrays Cauchon and the clerics as sober and conscientious men concerned for Joan's soul, it was later revealed by witnesses that most of them, Cauchon in particular, could barely conceal their glee. It was reported that they laughed as Cauchon told them, "You can have a great celebration, everything is prepared."

The next day—Tuesday, May 29—Cauchon and the other judges, doctors, lords, and masters assembled in the chapel of Rouen. Cauchon summarized the events of the preceding days, and one by one, each of the men present in the chapel voiced his opinion. They unanimously agreed that Joan should be condemned as a relapsed heretic and handed over to the secular authorities for execution.

May 30, 1431. The Last Day of the Trial

On the last day of May, early in the morning, Cauchon and the judges came to Joan's cell and asked one last time whether she had really seen the angels. A friar was summoned to hear her confession and administer the Eucharist.

Joan was brought in a cart to the Old Market for the final sentence to be pronounced before the people. Her head shaved bald, she wore a hat, like a dunce's cap, bearing the words "elapsed heretic, apostate, idolater." A final sermon was delivered by Master Nicolas Midi, Doctor of Theology, while Joan stood upon a platform in front of a "great multitude of people" gathered there.

The execution was carried out by the English. As the flames leapt up around Joan, a Dominican friar heeded her request and held a cross where she could see it. She was heard calling out the name of Jesus. The carnival mood of the crowd is said to have grown solemn, and one of King Henry's secretaries exclaimed, "We are lost! We have burned a saint." After her clothes had burned away, but before Joan's body was completely consumed, the debris was raked away to reveal that she was indeed a woman. When her body had burned completely, Joan's ashes were thrown into the Seine to prevent them from being buried in consecrated ground. Joan's executioner later stated that he was afraid he would be damned himself for having burned "a holy woman."

The Aftermath

Joan's fate was sealed once she told her Burgundian captors that it was God's will for the French to vanquish the English and drive them out of France. Four years after her martyrdom, the Duke of Burgundy and King Charles VII of France signed the Treaty of Arras, and in 1437, Charles rode triumphantly into Paris. The last English troops left France in 1450, and King Charles spoke publicly about Joan for the last time, asking the theologian Guillaume Bouille to look into the conduct of her trial. Charles feared that Joan's conviction as a lapsed heretic, in connection with her mission to put him on the throne, could raise questions about the legitimacy of his reign.

Though nineteen years had passed since Joan's trial, there were numerous witnesses who spoke of Cauchon taking orders from the English. One witness said that Cauchon had planted a spy with Burgundian leanings as Joan's confessor during her imprisonment. Several witnesses spoke of Joan having been subjected to sexual assault by her guards, and others testified to Joan's piety even as she burned. A list of articles was drawn up to serve as the basis for a retrial, or trial of rehabilitation, ordered by Pope Callixtus II. Among these articles were charges about the prejudice of the English, the lack of any legitimate legal counsel for Joan, and the grueling conditions of her interrogations.

The Trial of Rehabilitation

The retrial, held in Paris and overseen by three papal commissioners, attracted an enormous crowd. Joan's mother and other surviving family members were the plaintiffs, and numerous people who had known Joan as a child or followed her into battle testified. On July 7, 1456, the judges declared that the twelve articles brought against Joan during her trial were corrupt, deceitful, slanderous, fraudulent, and malicious, that her sentence was null and void, and that a cross should be erected at the spot where she had been burned in the Old Market of Rouen. The following year, Pope Callixtus excommunicated Bishop Pierre Cauchon (by then deceased) for his role in Joan's persecution and condemnation.

Canonization

Much of the testimony recorded during the trial of rehabilitation was used in the process of Joan's canonization, which didn't occur until nearly five hundred years later.

Joan of Arc was declared a saint in May of 1920 by Pope Benedict XV, who called her a "most brilliantly shining light of God." Her feast day is May 30, the date of her execution. She is recognized as the patron saint of France, martyrs, captives, prisoners, soldiers, military personnel (particularly women who have served), and those ridiculed for their piety.

Joan in Popular Culture

Long before Joan's canonization, she had become an iconic figure in French culture – the symbol of courage and French nationalism. In the years between her burning and her trial of rehabilitation, stories circulated intimating that Joan had miraculously survived the fire. There were even a number of women who claimed to be Joan, some of whom were rumored to have mystical powers. Joan's own brothers, Pierre and Jean, who had accompanied her into battle at Orléans, traveled around France with a woman purporting to be Joan of Arc and supported the imposter in her claims for six years. That woman, Claude des Armoises, later known as Jeanne des Armoires, apparently had Pierre and Jean fooled initially, though there is plenty of reason to believe that they kept up the charade for most of those six years because they received gifts wherever they went. Claude was unmasked when she met King Charles VII and was unable to repeat the "secret" Joan had told him to convince the dauphin that she had been sent by God to defeat the English.

Though Joan fell out of favor during the French Revolution for her close association with the French monarchy, her image has been carried into battle by generation upon generation of French soldiers, sailors, and airmen. Her deeds and fate have inspired poets, dramatists, authors, and artists of all types. The nineteen-minute-long French silent film *Jeanne d'Arc* (1900) is a romanticized depiction of Joan's life, ending with a scene in which she ascends into heaven and is greeted by God and her saints. Perhaps the best-known film about the life of Joan of Arc was the 1948 film directed by Victor Fleming that starred Ingrid Bergman in an adaptation of Maxwell Anderson's Broadway play, *Joan of Lorraine.* In 1967, Genevieve Bujold played the title role in an American Hallmark Hall of Fame adaptation of George Bernard Shaw's play *Saint Joan.* Mark Twain, though an avowed anti-Catholic and critic of the French, referred to her as "by far the most extraordinary person the human race has ever produced." There have been many more tributes to her faith and heroism over the years. Joan even appeared as a character in 1989's *Bill & Ted's Excellent Adventure!*

But if Joan was ever painted or sketched during her lifetime, no such image has survived. The only contemporary depiction of the Maid was a sketch created by someone who had never seen her. What we do have is the most extensive documentation of the life and deeds of any medieval peasant woman who ever lived. From the transcripts and correspondence generated during her trial has emerged a persona that millions, Catholics and non-Catholics alike, have come to regard as the embodiment of courage and faith.

Printed in Great Britain
by Amazon

64283881R00071